Original title:
Silent Strength

Copyright © 2024 Swan Charm
All rights reserved.

Author: Daisy Dewi
ISBN HARDBACK: 978-9916-89-930-4
ISBN PAPERBACK: 978-9916-89-931-1
ISBN EBOOK: 978-9916-89-932-8

In the Shadows, I Stand

In quiet dusk, where whispers dwell,
I find my soul in broken shell.
The light may fade, but strength will rise,
As faith ignites the darkened skies.

With every trial, my heart does swell,
A silent prayer, a sacred spell.
Though shadows creep and doubts demand,
In peace I wait, in grace I stand.

The Hushed Testament

In solemn silence, truth unfolds,
A story bright, though softly told.
Each heart, a witness to the light,
In every loss, a new insight.

With gentle hands, we mold our fate,
In love's embrace, we find our state.
The whispers of the past resound,
In humble hearts, our hope is found.

The Refuge of the Resolute

In storms of doubt, I seek the calm,
Where hope is held, a healing balm.
A fortress built on faith and grace,
In trials faced, I find my place.

With steadfast heart, I walk the way,
Through darkest nights and brightest day.
The resolute shall never wane,
For in their courage, love will reign.

A Gentle Force

With open arms, a spirit pure,
A gentle force that will endure.
In every kindness, love's refrain,
The quiet strength that breaks the chain.

In tender grace, the weak are strong,
United souls, we all belong.
The power found in softest sighs,
A shared embrace, where mercy lies.

Resilience in the Veil of Night

In shadows deep, we find our way,
With faith that guides, both night and day.
Through trials fierce, our spirits rise,
A beacon bright, beneath dark skies.

The whispers soft, of dreams anew,
In quiet moments, hope breaks through.
With every tear, a lesson learned,
The fires of strength, within us burned.

The stars above, they gently gleam,
A promise held within the dream.
Through storms of doubt, we bravely tread,
In love's embrace, we're safely led.

The night may cloak, our path in gray,
But hearts ablaze, we find our way.
With every heartbeat, courage grows,
In the veil of night, resilience glows.

We gather strength, from those before,
Their stories weave, a sacred lore.
In unity, we stand as one,
A tapestry of hope begun.

The Gossamer Threads of Hope

In every dawn, a promise made,
The light that breaks, the past must fade.
With fragile threads, of dreams and grace,
We weave our fate, in time and space.

Each whispered prayer, a sacred sound,
In troubled times, our hearts are bound.
With every breath, new life we claim,
In love's embrace, we rise in flame.

Through valleys low, we seek the high,
Our spirits soar, like birds on high.
Each thread of hope, a guiding star,
Through life's vast sea, no dream too far.

In gentle rains, our sorrows cleanse,
The gossamer threads, our soul defends.
With each setback, we grow more strong,
In unity, we'll sing our song.

With open hearts, we face the day,
In faith and love, we find our way.
The threads of hope, forever spun,
Together strong, as one we run.

Shadows of Divine Resilience

In the valley of sorrow, we find our way,
With whispers of grace that guide each day.
Through trials and anguish, our spirits rise,
For in shadows of darkness, true strength lies.

Hope springs eternal, a radiant seed,
Nurtured by faith in times of need.
In silence we gather, our hearts entwined,
With the shadows of resilience, our souls aligned.

The Gentle Hand of Providence

In the quiet moments, a touch so near,
The gentle hand of Providence calms our fear.
With each breath taken, a promise assured,
In valleys of doubt, our faith is secured.

Through storms and tempests, we find our peace,
Embraced by love that will never cease.
In the tapestry woven, each thread divine,
The gentle hand of Providence, our lifeline.

The Quiet Light of Hope

In the darkest hour, a flicker remains,
The quiet light of hope breaks the chains.
Guiding our steps through the shadows around,
In the stillness we find where love is found.

With each rising dawn, new dreams take flight,
Illuminating souls with celestial light.
Together we blossom, united, we cope,
Holding close the quiet, the radiant hope.

Emblems of Endurance in the Dark

In the depths of despair, strength takes its stand,
Emblems of endurance, by faith's gentle hand.
Though trials may tremble, we rise like the dawn,
In the embrace of the night, our spirits are drawn.

With courage like mountains, unyielding and proud,
We stand in the silence, resolute and loud.
For in every struggle, a vision ignites,
Emblems of endurance, our souls' shining lights.

A Flame Without Sound

In silence, a flame does rise,
Glowing softly 'neath the skies.
Its warmth a gift, unspoken prayer,
Kindling hope, everywhere.

Guided by a gentle force,
It lights the night, a sacred course.
In whispers, it dances bright,
A beacon found in darkest night.

Flickering truth in hearts aglow,
A tender warmth, a sacred flow.
It sways within the mind's embrace,
A silent guide, a holy grace.

Though unseen, its presence strong,
In every soul, it sings a song.
With flickers bold, it breaks the ground,
The spirit's dance, a flame profound.

In deep stillness, it will thrive,
A quiet light, our hopes revive.
No need for words, just heart's intent,
In silent faith, love's flame is spent.

The Voice of the Inner Light

A whisper rings within the soul,
Echoes soft, to make us whole.
In shadowed paths, it leads the way,
Guiding hearts where truth may sway.

Each breath a prayer, soft and low,
In the stillness, visions flow.
A chorus played on heartstrings taut,
In every silence, wisdom sought.

With every step, its presence calls,
A melody that never falls.
Through trials faced and mountains high,
The inner light will never die.

Awake to thoughts that softly shine,
In sacred stillness, hearts align.
The voice of love in each heartbeat,
In every moment, holiness meet.

From depths of darkness, softly rise,
With every breath, to touch the skies.
The inner journey, a sacred rite,
We find our peace in inner light.

Hidden Warriors of Grace

In shadows deep, the warriors stand,
Guardians wrought by Heaven's hand.
With silent strength, they face the storm,
Their spirits fierce, yet hearts are warm.

They carry faith like armor bright,
In battles fought within the night.
Though unseen by the worldly eye,
Their courage soars, like eagles high.

With every challenge, hope they find,
Their gentle ways, though undefined.
In whispers soft, they share their creed,
To heal the heart, fulfill the need.

Each tear they shed, a sacred seed,
A testament to love's true deed.
Through trials faced, their light will shine,
In every act, divine design.

Though hidden, they will always rise,
With grace adorned, they touch the skies.
Unyielding faith, their silent hymn,
The hidden warriors, hearts so brim.

In the Depths of Solitude

In silence deep, the spirit breathes,
Amongst the trees, the stillness weaves.
A sacred space where time stands still,
In solitude, the heart can fill.

The echoes of the soul's refrain,
In quiet whispers, peace we gain.
Each moment spent in still retreat,
In depths unseen, we find our seat.

With every shadow softly cast,
The burdens lift, the trials past.
In quietude, we hear the call,
The truth revealed, a gentle thrall.

Though alone, our hearts entwined,
In solitude, the divine aligned.
The sacred dance of presence found,
In the depths, our love unbound.

Rejoice in stillness, sweet embrace,
In solitude, we find our grace.
In every breath, life's song resounds,
In the depths of silence, love abounds.

Serenity's Sacred Song

In quiet chambers, whispers flow,
A melody of peace we know.
With gentle grace, the soul aligns,
In sacred light, our heart entwines.

The stars above, a guiding light,
As day surrenders into night.
Each breath we take, a prayer defined,
In tranquil trust, our path we find.

With every tear, a lesson learned,
In stillness, love's bright lantern burned.
Through trials faced, we rise anew,
With faith as strong as morning dew.

In nature's arms, we seek our way,
The sacred song will never stray.
For in the hush, we come to see,
The joy of simply being free.

Unyielding Faith in the Midst of Storms

When tempest rages and darkness calls,
We stand as one, no fear befalls.
With unwavering hearts, we paddle forth,
In faith we trust, our true north.

The winds may howl, the skies may weep,
Yet in our souls, a promise deep.
Through trials fierce, we make our stand,
With courage lent by faith's own hand.

Each drop of rain, a testament,
Of love unchained, of hearts well spent.
In midst of chaos, we find our grace,
As steadfast spirits embrace the space.

With every wave that crashes down,
We wear the storm like a sacred crown.
For even in the darkest hour,
We find within our deepest power.

The Unbreakable Spirit

Through shadows cast and trials faced,
A light within, our hearts embraced.
Though burdens heavy, we shall rise,
In every struggle, spirit flies.

With every stumble, strength we find,
A beacon bright, our spirits aligned.
With laughter shared, with love's embrace,
We fuel our fire, we quicken pace.

No chains can bind a heart that's free,
In every moment, grace we see.
As storms do pass, the sun will shine,
In unity, our spirits entwine.

With hope anew, we greet each dawn,
The unbreakable spirit carries on.
For in the depths of every fight,
We rise again, emboldened light.

Foundations in the Stillness

In quiet pause, foundations grow,
The stillness speaks, we come to know.
In whispers soft, the truths take flight,
A sanctuary, heart ignites.

With every breath, serenity blooms,
In silence vast, creation looms.
As thoughts align, we claim our space,
In grounded trust, we find our grace.

Through life's great storms, we stand as one,
With open hearts, we seek the sun.
In humble moments, strength is found,
As echoes rise, love knows no bound.

In stillness deep, we learn to see,
The sacred thread that binds you and me.
Within this peace, we find our call,
The journey shared, our souls enthrall.

The Light that Binds in Quietude

In the stillness, light descends,
Whispers gentle, truth transcends.
Hearts unite in silent grace,
Graceful shadows, love's embrace.

Each moment pure, a sacred thread,
Woven softly, where angels tread.
In quietude, our spirits soar,
A divine echo, forevermore.

Hand in hand, we seek the way,
Guided by the light to stay.
Beyond the noise, the harmony,
In quietude, we find the key.

The world awakens, souls align,
In every breath, the great design.
From silence springs a cosmic song,
Together we are safe and strong.

With every pulse, the light grows bright,
In darkness, faith becomes our sight.
The light that binds, a sacred bond,
In stillness deep, we journey on.

Prayers of the Invisible Warrior

In the shadows, silent plea,
Invisible strength, we must see.
Fighting battles, hearts ignite,
With faith as armor, we unite.

Each whispered prayer brings forth light,
Guiding us through endless night.
Courage blooms in secret sighs,
As the spirit learns to rise.

Through the storm, a warrior's grace,
In unseen realms, we find our place.
Bold and fierce, yet tender too,
In prayerful strength, we are renewed.

The glory rests in humble hearts,
In every tear, a brand new start.
Invisible echoes, loud and clear,
We stand together, free from fear.

Let faith be our battle cry,
On wings of hope, we learn to fly.
With every prayer, we pave the way,
Invisible warriors, come what may.

The Sacred Dance of Solitude

In solitude, the spirit sings,
A dance of peace that presence brings.
Each heartbeat marks the time and place,
In stillness, we behold His grace.

Twisting shadows, candlelight,
The sacred dance, a gentle sight.
In moments hushed, our souls align,
With every step, the heart divine.

Whirling softly, hearts enshrine,
In solitude, our love will shine.
Lost in wonder, found in awe,
In each embrace, we feel the law.

The world outside may fade away,
In the heart's chamber, we will stay.
The sacred rhythm of the mind,
In dancing feet, new joy we find.

Awake anew in quiet's fold,
In sacred dance, the truth unfolds.
Where solitude and love entwine,
A tranquil space where souls define.

Through the Veil of Quietude

Through the veil, a whisper flows,
In quietude, the spirit knows.
Gentle touch of sacred time,
In silence deep, all hearts will rhyme.

Moments pass like autumn leaves,
In soft embrace, the spirit grieves.
Yet from the stillness, strength will rise,
With open hands, we seek the skies.

The quiet holds a wisdom rare,
In every breath, a fervent prayer.
Through hidden paths, the light will gleam,
In tranquil waters, we'll redeem.

Veiled in layers of sacred trust,
In unity, we find what's just.
The echoes linger, soft and clear,
Through tranquil tones, His love draws near.

In endless quiet, truth revives,
Through the veil, the spirit thrives.
Embrace the stillness, let it guide,
Through quietude, we abide.

A Solid Ground Beneath Tranquility

In silent whispers, peace does grow,
A solid ground where calm winds blow.
Beneath the heavens, stars align,
In tranquil shadows, light divine.

With faith, we walk this sacred land,
In every heart, a gentle hand.
The burdens lifted, spirits soar,
With love, we seek forevermore.

The rivers flow as grace bestows,
In every heart, the spirit knows.
A gentle touch, a guiding star,
In harmony, we journey far.

When troubles rise, His whispers near,
A solid ground dispels our fear.
In every trial, His promise stands,
Our hearts united as He plans.

We stand as one, in prayers we weave,
With open hearts, we shall believe.
In tranquil peace, His light we find,
A solid ground where love is blind.

The Immovable Heart

In storms of life, my heart remains,
A steadfast soul through joys and pains.
With faith unshaken, strong and bright,
It holds the flame, a guiding light.

When shadows creep and doubts arise,
The heart, unmoved, to truth denies.
With every beat, a sacred vow,
To love the world, to praise the now.

Through trials deep and rivers wide,
With grace to lead, I shall abide.
In every tear, a seed of hope,
The immovable heart will cope.

Its love transcends, the barriers break,
In every choice, a chance we take.
Embracing all, in peace we find,
The beauty in the ties that bind.

In quiet strength, it stands apart,
The world may shake, but not the heart.
In faith, we rise, though shadows fall,
The immovable heart, it binds us all.

Echoes of Endurance

Through valleys low and mountains high,
The echoes of our faith reply.
In every voice, a hymn of grace,
Enduring love, our saving place.

When darkness looms and fears arise,
We raise our eyes to endless skies.
The whispers of the past resound,
In echoes deep, our strength is found.

With every heartbeat, resilient song,
In trials faced, we shall be strong.
The whispers call, as hope in flight,
In echoes wide, our spirits light.

Embrace the struggle, let it teach,
In shadows cast, we learn to reach.
Through every storm, through endless fight,
Our echoes sing of strength and light.

For every test, a promise made,
In love's embrace, we won't be swayed.
With courage born from ancient tides,
Echoes of endurance, our hearts guide.

A Fortress Hidden in Grace

In stillness found, we build our place,
A fortress strong, hidden in grace.
With every prayer, our walls arise,
Encased in truth, beneath the skies.

Through trials fierce and tempests bold,
Within this heart, a warmth to hold.
The whispers soft, a gentle shield,
A fortress built through love revealed.

With every tear, a stone is laid,
In bonds of faith, we will not fade.
In unity, our spirits soar,
A fortress standing evermore.

When darkness falls, our light shines bright,
Within this home, we find our sight.
The strength of hearts, a sacred space,
A fortress safe, all wrapped in grace.

So let us gather, side by side,
With open arms and hearts as guide.
In love's embrace, we hold the key,
A fortress built on unity.

A Silken Shield of Faith

In the stillness of dawn's embrace,
Faith whispers softly in the heart.
A silken shield, gentle and warm,
Guarding the soul, never to part.

Through trials fierce, the spirit stands,
With woven threads of hope and love.
In shadows cast by doubt's dark hand,
The light of grace descends from above.

Each prayer a stitch, in trust we weave,
A tapestry of dreams and light.
In quietude, we learn to believe,
That faith will guide us through the night.

With every tear, a lesson learned,
Each moment, like a precious gem.
From ashes rise, the spirit churned,
In strength anew, we find our zen.

Embrace the dawn with open eyes,
For every breath is life's sweet gift.
In the realm of the unseen skies,
A silken shield, our faith will lift.

The Quiet Guardian

In the silence, a gentle breath,
A guardian watches over all.
With eyes that see beyond the strife,
It catches every teardrop's fall.

Within the heart, a peace resides,
A quiet strength, steadfast and true.
It shields the weary, heals the pain,
With whispers soft that renew.

Through stormy skies and darkest nights,
This guardian stands, unwavering.
With each heartbeat, it ignites
A flicker of hope, not fading.

In the tapestry of fate we weave,
Its threads of love are ever near.
A promise made, in faith we cleave,
A path of light, no room for fear.

With open arms, the quiet call,
A presence felt in every prayer.
In every soul, a guardian's thrall,
Guiding all with tender care.

Unseen Vows of Valor

In the heart's deep chamber lies,
A vow unspoken, yet so bold.
Through trials faced and fears defied,
Unseen valor, a tale retold.

Each step we take upon the earth,
Is etched with courage, pure and true.
In shadows deep, we find our worth,
With silent strength, we push on through.

The bonds we forge, though hidden tight,
Inspire the weary, lift the weak.
In every challenge, we ignite,
A light within, no words we speak.

Through storms that rage and tempests loud,
Our spirits rise like eagles soar.
In unity, we form the crowd,
To lift each other evermore.

In unseen vows, we find our grace,
With hearts entwined, we stand as one.
In every struggle we embrace,
We rise together, never done.

The Strength of Timid Hands

In gentle whispers, courage blooms,
Timid hands reach out to hold.
They weave a path through life's rough rooms,
With strength that's quiet, yet so bold.

In moments fraught with doubts and fears,
These hands have mended broken things.
With every gesture, love appears,
A symphony of hope it sings.

Though small in size, they bear the weight,
Of every heart they choose to touch.
In kindness, they can alter fate,
Empowering souls, oh, so much.

Through trials faced and battles won,
The timid hands become the might.
In every dawn, a new hour spun,
They grasp the light and banish night.

So let them rise and take their stand,
For in their quiet, strength is found.
A testament of life so grand,
Timid hands reach out, unbound.

Whispers of the Steadfast Heart

In the silence of the night, they speak,
Echoes of hope in darkness, so meek.
Trust weaves a tapestry of light,
Guiding our souls to the divine height.

Faithful shadows dance in prayer,
Cloaked in grace, without a care.
Beneath the burdens, love resides,
In every tear, the spirit abides.

Through trials fierce and fears that bind,
A gentle whisper calms the mind.
The steadfast heart, though tried and sore,
Rises again, believing more.

In every heartbeat, a promise shines,
Connected souls across the lines.
United in the quest for peace,
In whispered bonds, our worries cease.

So let us walk through valleys deep,
With faith that never falls asleep.
The steadfast heart shall find its rest,
In love's embrace, forever blessed.

The Hidden Fortress of Faith

In shadows cast by doubt and fear,
A fortress stands, ever near.
Walls of prayer, strong and tall,
Against the storms, they will not fall.

Through trials deep, we seek the keep,
Where promises are ours to reap.
Each stone laid with hope anew,
A shelter safe, forever true.

In quiet moments, grace descends,
A mighty force that always bends.
In every prayer, a steadfast stone,
Together, never walk alone.

The hidden fortress, our sacred ground,
In unity, our strength is found.
With every step in faith we take,
Stronger still, the ground we make.

So let the winds of change arise,
In the fortress, our spirits rise.
Within these walls, we find our place,
In faith's embrace, we sing His grace.

Unseen Armor Against the Storm

When tempests roar and shadows loom,
With unseen armor, we face the gloom.
A shield of faith, a sword of light,
In battles fierce, we stand upright.

Each trial faced, a lesson learned,\nIn every heart, a fire burned.
With courage clad, we march ahead,
Trusting the path our Savior led.

Through raging storms that test our will,
With steadfast hearts, we climb each hill.
In whispers soft, the truth proclaimed,
The unseen armor, forever named.

Every struggle makes us strong,
In unity, we sing our song.
For in His might, we find our way,
Unseen but felt, come what may.

So let the storms begin their play,
With unseen strength, we'll never sway.
For armor gifted from above,
Shields us in His endless love.

Veils of Quiet Resolve

In the stillness of our prayers, we find,
Veils that cover hearts entwined.
Quiet resolve, a gentle might,
Guiding spirits in the night.

Each whisper soft, a sacred thought,
In peace, the battles bravely fought.
With every breath, we seek His face,
Wrapped in love, we find our place.

Through trials faced, and joys embraced,
The quiet resolve cannot be replaced.
In moments frail, our strength renewed,
A bond that cannot be subdued.

So here we stand, hand in hand,
With faith that knows, we understand.
In all that life may throw our way,
Our quiet resolve forever shall stay.

In every step, His light we trace,
Veils of hope across this space.
In gentle strength, we find our voice,
In quiet resolve, we rejoice.

A Song of Inner Fortitude

In shadows deep, my spirit stands,
With faith as strong as ancient bands.
Through trials fierce, I seek the light,
The strength within, my heart's true sight.

Though storms may rage and fears may rise,
I hold my ground, I touch the skies.
With every breath, a vow renewed,
In silent prayers, my soul is stewed.

The path ahead is oft unclear,
Yet in my heart, I cast out fear.
For courage is a sacred flame,
That burns within, forever tame.

I rise above the doubt and pain,
With grace bestowed, I break the chain.
Each step I take, with purpose bright,
I walk in peace, I walk in light.

So sing I now, my hymn of praise,
To all who fight through darkest days.
For in our hearts, the truth we find,
The inner strength that's truly blind.

The Refuge of Quiet Waters

In tranquil streams, the spirit glows,
Where gentle whispers calm the throes.
The silence speaks, in tender grace,
A refuge found, a sacred place.

As ripples dance beneath the trees,
The heart can rest; it finds its ease.
In quiet shores, the mind may roam,
To find the strength to call it home.

Each drop reflects the light divine,
In every wave, a peace we find.
The world may roar, yet here, we stay,
In quiet waters, come what may.

As moments pass like fleeting clouds,
I breathe the stillness, free from crowds.
Within this space, my soul takes flight,
In sacred calm, I see the light.

So may we seek these waters clear,
To soothe the heart and calm the fear.
For every soul deserves a chance,
To find the peace in nature's dance.

The Unshaken Stone

In tempest's roar, the stone does stand,
Unmoved by force, by fate's strong hand.
Through trials fierce, it does not yield,
A testament upon the field.

Time flows and ebbs, yet it remains,
A silent watcher of joys and pains.
Each crack a story, each mark a sign,
Of steadfast love that's pure, divine.

The storms may come, the winds may wail,
But in its core, the truth prevails.
With every challenge, it grows more grand,
A fortress held by nature's hand.

So let us learn from this firm stone,
To face our fears, to stand alone.
In trials faced, we find our grace,
And carve our names in time and space.

With steady hearts, we venture forth,
Embracing all that life brings forth.
For like the stone, we too can rise,
Unshaken by the darkest skies.

The Whispers of Resilience

In every heart, a whisper sings,
Of strength concealed within our wings.
Through darkest nights and brightest days,
Resilience weaves its timeless ways.

The trials faced, the burdens borne,
In every ache, a hope is worn.
The spirit bends but does not break,
A silent vow that we will make.

From ashes rise, like phoenix bold,
In every story, life unfolds.
With gentle hands, we craft our fate,
In whispers soft, we cultivate.

Each moment lived, a lesson clear,
With every fall, we persevere.
For in the struggle, strength is found,
A sacred bond, forever bound.

So listen close, to that sweet sound,
Of whispered tales where hope is found.
For in our hearts, we hold the key,
To rise again, resiliently.

The Stronghold of Resilience

In trials fierce, we stand and pray,
With courage bright, we find our way.
Our hearts are strong, our spirits keen,
In faith, we've built our sturdy sheen.

From ashes rise, a spirit bold,
Through raging storms, our strength unfolds.
Each setback holds a seed of grace,
In every wound, a sacred space.

Together we shall face the night,
With hope as armor, hearts alight.
The stronghold built on love's embrace,
Will guide us through, our sacred place.

Though shadows loom, we shall not fall,
In unity, we hear the call.
With faithful hearts, we brave the fight,
Resilience shines, a guiding light.

Through trials vast, our stories blend,
In every hurt, our souls transcend.
For in the depths, we learn to rise,
Resilience leads to brighter skies.

The Softness of Faith

In quiet whispers, gentle grace,
We find the love in every space.
With tender hearts, we seek to feel,
The soothing touch, our wounds to heal.

Faith flows like rivers, soft and deep,
In sacred silence, our souls keep.
A hush that speaks, a song divine,
In moments frail, our hearts align.

Through trials wide, and pains we bear,
In softness found, there's strength to share.
Each tear a prayer, each sigh a song,
In faith's embrace, we all belong.

As petals fall, and seasons change,
In every loss, there's beauty strange.
The softness of our faith will guide,
With open hearts, we walk beside.

In gentle dawns, we find our way,
With faith as sunlight, brightening the day.
No harsher truth than love's pure breath,
In softness laid, we conquer death.

The Lantern in the Dark

In shadows deep, a light will spark,
A guiding flame, a faithful mark.
With every step, we draw the near,
The lantern glows, dispelling fear.

As night descends, our hearts ignite,
In darkest hours, we find the light.
Through every pain, and trials stark,
The lantern shines, a hopeful arc.

Each flicker tells a tale of grace,
Of love's embrace, a warm embrace.
In every heart, a spark resides,
The lantern leads as darkness hides.

With open hands, we lift our gaze,
To stars above, the light arrays.
In unity, our spirits soar,
The lantern's glow forevermore.

Through winding roads, the journey's long,
Yet in our hearts, we sing this song.
For love's pure light shall always hark,
To guide us home, this lantern spark.

The Strength Found in Silence

In silence sweet, the spirit speaks,
In tranquil rooms, our heartache leaks.
Each breath a prayer, a stillness sought,
In muted grace, our battles fought.

The quiet wisdom, deep and vast,
In moments still, our souls hold fast.
Through whispered thoughts, we come to see,
In peaceful hearts, our spirits free.

When words are few, the truth unfolds,
In silence pure, the heart beholds.
A strength erupts from deep within,
In stillness found, our lives begin.

Through storms of noise, we seek the calm,
In gentle rest, we find the balm.
For in the hush, our courage gleams,
The strength resides within our dreams.

Embrace the silence, let it flow,
In quietude, our spirits grow.
For strength is found in places bare,
In sacred stillness, love is rare.

Stars of Hope in Midnight's Embrace

In darkest night, the stars do gleam,
With whispers soft, they light our dream.
Each twinkle sings of love divine,
Guiding souls through paths entwined.

When shadows loom and fears arise,
The heavens grant their sacred guise.
Every spark, a prayer unspoken,
In silence bound, our hearts are broken.

Though tempests roar and winds dismay,
The stars will show the way, we pray.
In midnight's clasp, our spirits rise,
With every heartbeat, hope defies.

For every tear, a star will shine,
Transcending pain, we seek divine.
The cosmos' dance, a verse of grace,
In darkness found, light takes its place.

The Subtle Hand of Providence

Upon the winds, a soft caress,
Invisible hands in our distress.
Through trials faced and burdens borne,
A guiding presence, never worn.

In every choice, a purpose clear,
The quiet voice that calms our fear.
Through joy and pain, through loss and gain,
The hand unseen, our hearts sustain.

When paths are fraught with doubt and strife,
The gentle touch restores our life.
In moments meek, a strength revealed,
The subtle hand that wounds can heal.

So trust the weave of fate's embrace,
In every bruise, a touch of grace.
For life's design, though dark and bright,
Is crafted by a hand of light.

The Serenity of Endangered Dreams

In whispered hopes where shadows dwell,
A sacred space where hearts can swell.
Each dream, a seed, in peril sown,
Yet brave and bold, we stand alone.

The world may shake, but spirit stays,
In fragile hearts, the ember plays.
With every sigh, our wishes soar,
In sacred trust, we yearn for more.

Though tempest winds may seek to steal,
The quiet strength that we conceal.
For dreams, though endangered, never fade,
In love's embrace, they are remade.

So gather close, our dreams unite,
In every struggle, find the light.
With hope renewed, our journey gleams,
Through faith, we hold our valued dreams.

Tempered by Trials, Forged in Grace

Through fires deep, our spirits grow,
In trials faced, we learn to know.
With every test, a strength emerges,
In darkest nights, our fervor surges.

For grace awaits where hearts abide,
In humbled souls, divine will guide.
Through weary paths, we find our way,
Like rivers flow, we bend, we sway.

The trials faced, each scar a tale,
In joy and pain, we shall not fail.
For every burden lifts our soul,
In faith's embrace, we become whole.

So trust the journey, close and dear,
Each step a sacred path sincere.
For tempered hearts, with grace adorned,
Shall rise anew, forever warmed.

The Unyielding Foundation of the Heart

In shadows deep, where faith takes root,
A whisper calls, like angels' lute.
Through trials fierce, it stands so bold,
The heart, a fortress, love's pure gold.

From ashes rise, to skies so blue,
With grace untold, the spirit grew.
In every tear, a lesson learned,
The fire ignites, the heart's yearned.

With every beat, the truth unfolds,
In kindness wrapped, like purest gold.
A purpose shines, a guiding star,
In unity, we rise from far.

With hands entwined, we walk the path,
In sacred trust, we find the math.
Each step we take, in love we dwell,
A journey blessed, where spirits swell.

As dawn breaks forth, the light ascends,
In hope we trust, our soul defends.
The unyielding heart, a song so bright,
In faith we rest, by grace's light.

Threads of Courage Woven in Quiet

In silence deep, where hearts convene,
A gentle strength, serene yet keen.
The threads of courage, soft yet strong,
Woven with love, the endless song.

Each whispered prayer, a silent plea,
In darkened hours, we seek to see.
With every breath, a promise made,
In quiet trust, our fears we'll trade.

Through storms of doubt, the heart remains,
Resilient spirit, through the pains.
The tapestry of grace unfolds,
In threads of hope, our fate consoles.

Unseen by many, yet felt so deep,
In shadows cast, our spirits leap.
Together bound, in faith we rise,
Through woven threads, we touch the skies.

With courage found, we walk the line,
In quiet strength, our souls align.
Threads of courage, a journey vast,
A woven tale from first to last.

Strength Embodied in Reverent Stillness

In stillness deep, where sorrows cease,
A strength emerges, a quiet peace.
In moments hushed, the spirit stirs,
Embodying grace, as silence blurs.

Each breath we take, a prayer in time,
In reverence, we find the rhyme.
The strength that swells within the soul,
A steady force that makes us whole.

Through trials faced, in calm we stand,
With open hearts and reaching hands.
In unity, our spirits bind,
A strength within, forever kind.

The world may rush, but we will pause,
In sacred stillness, we find our cause.
With hearts attuned to love's embrace,
Strength embodied in this holy space.

In quiet corners, where shadows play,
We gather light to guide our way.
In reverent stillness, we shall see,
The strength that lies in you and me.

The Hidden Garden of Serenity

In secret glades where whispers bloom,
A hidden garden dispels the gloom.
With tender hands, we plant the seeds,
Of peace and love, the heart's true needs.

Among the branches, sunlight beams,
In every leaf, a gentle dream.
A tapestry of colors bright,
The garden thrives in sacred light.

With every flower, a story told,
Of hope and grace, in petals bold.
In stillness found, the spirit plays,
In this divine, enchanted maze.

The fragrance sweet, of love's embrace,
In every corner, a sacred place.
The hidden garden, where hearts belong,
In unity, we sing our song.

So come, dear friend, and find the door,
To nature's heart, forevermore.
In the hidden garden, we shall see,
Serenity's gift, a legacy.

The Silent Keeper of Dreams

In the quiet shadows, dreams take flight,
A guardian watches through the night.
Softly weaving hopes so bright,
Each whisper a promise in gentle light.

With every sigh, the heart speaks low,
Underneath the stars' soft glow.
In silence, the soul learns to know,
That dreams are seeds we tenderly sow.

In the stillness, we find our way,
Guided by faith, we choose to stay.
Embracing the dawn of a new day,
Where the keeper dwells, come what may.

Hearts entwined in a sacred quest,
Finding solace in moments blessed.
Each vision's truth, a gentle test,
In the keeper's arms, we find our rest.

So let us dream with open eyes,
For in the night, hope never dies.
In the silent keeper, love complies,
Breathing life where the heart relies.

Wisdom in the Whispering Wind

In the breeze that stirs the trees,
Lies a wisdom carried with ease.
Softly speaking through the leaves,
Nature's secrets the heart believes.

Each gust a voice, a calling clear,
Reminding us that hope is near.
In the stillness, we draw near,
To hear the whispers we hold dear.

Through valleys low and mountains high,
The wind conveys the reasons why.
In its embrace, we learn to fly,
Casting worries like clouds on the sky.

With every breath, a lesson flows,
In every rustle, the spirit grows.
Through the whispers, the heart knows,
The path to peace that gently glows.

Let the wisdom in the wind guide,
Trust in the journey, love beside.
With every sigh, we turn the tide,
Finding strength in the soft, sweet ride.

A Gentle Roar of Hope

In the stillness, a whisper strong,
Echoes promise, where we belong.
A gentle roar, a heart's sweet song,
Reminding us that we are not wrong.

With every struggle, strength is born,
In the dark hours, we are reborn.
Through the clouds, the light is worn,
A gentle roar that greets the morn.

Through trials faced, the spirit bends,
In unity, our courage mends.
With every heartbeat, love transcends,
A gentle roar that never ends.

So let us rise, our voices blend,
A chorus of hope that we defend.
In our hearts, the truths commend,
The gentle roar, our faithful friend.

With every dawn, new dreams unfold,
In the warmth of stories told.
A gentle roar, a heart of gold,
Embracing love in peace, so bold.

The Sanctity of Inner Peace

In the chamber of the heart, a light,
Illuminates the path to right.
In silence rests the sacred might,
Where chaos bows, and souls take flight.

Within the stillness, a voice is found,
A gentle echo, a healing sound.
In this peace, all fears unbound,
Transcending limits, we are crowned.

Beneath the shadows, serenely tread,
Through trials faced, the spirit led.
In every tear, a prayer is said,
Finding solace where hope is fed.

With every breath, we weave a prayer,
In the sanctuary, we lay bare.
Finding grace in the view we share,
In unity, we learn to care.

So let our hearts awaken wide,
Embracing peace as our true guide.
In the depths, let love abide,
The sanctity of self inside.

Still Waters Run Deep

In stillness, grace begins to flow,
A quiet heart knows depths below.
Whispers soft in sacred space,
The soul's embrace, a warm, sweet place.

Beneath the surface, truths reside,
In silence, faith and love abide.
Glistening ripples tell the tale,
Of hope that sings when all seems pale.

The gentle stream, a guide divine,
Reflects the light, so pure, so fine.
In every droplet, blessings greet,
The solace found in waters sweet.

When troubled skies obscure the view,
The stillness speaks, and brings us through.
Trust in the depths, where peace is sown,
For in those waters, we are known.

With every breath, the calm remains,
Soft whispers wash away the pains.
Still waters run, and we must keep,
In faith we walk, where love runs deep.

The Hidden Pillar

A pillar stands where few can see,
In quiet strength, it holds the key.
Beneath the weight of burdens worn,
It stands steadfast, though oft forlorn.

Behind the scenes, it guards the way,
A hidden guide that won't decay.
Though shadows cloak its silent grace,
In every heart, it finds a place.

With roots deep set in sacred ground,
Its whispers lift the lost and bound.
Through trials fierce, it will not bend,
The pillar strong, our faithful friend.

In every storm, it anchors true,
A silent witness, tried and new.
In humbleness, it stands alone,
The beacon light, our cornerstone.

So let us seek beyond the veil,
The steadfast love where we prevail.
For in the quiet, strength we find,
The hidden pillar, kind and blind.

A Prayer in the Shadows

In shadows cast by worldly haste,
A prayer is born, so sweetly placed.
With whispered hopes, we seek the light,
In darkness deep, our souls take flight.

A flicker shines in midnight's gaze,
As silent hearts begin to praise.
In humble corners, faith ignites,
A sacred bond, no fear ignites.

The stars align in quiet grace,
Illuminating every space.
Each echo soft, a gentle breath,
A prayer that conquers fear and death.

In shadows deep, love's warmth we find,
A sacred rhythm, intertwined.
In every moment, hope prevails,
As we embrace the love that hails.

So let us pray when night descends,
For in those shadows, light ascends.
A prayer that echoes through the years,
With every word, we cast our fears.

The Strength of Gentle Hands

In gentle hands, the strength we find,
A tender touch, a heart aligned.
With open palms, they weave a tale,
Of love that lifts, where others fail.

A soothing balm for wounds unseen,
In quiet moments, grace may glean.
For every gesture, soft and kind,
A testament to hope combined.

With every grasp, a bond is formed,
In unity, our spirits warmed.
The gentle touch, a healer's art,
Restores the weary, stirs the heart.

When storm clouds gather, fears arise,
The strength of love, it never dies.
In every hug, in every hold,
A story of the brave and bold.

So let us cherish gentle ways,
And through the night, let kindness blaze.
For strength revealed in tenderness,
Is where we find our truest rest.

In gentle hands, we trust and see,
The power found in harmony.
A strength divine, forever grand,
In every heart, a gentle hand.

The Unseen Waves of Faith

In shadows deep, where light does fade,
A whisper stirs, hope's serenade.
Silent tides, they ebb and flow,
Unseen grace, we come to know.

Through storms that rage and doubts that rise,
Faith anchors hearts, unseen, it ties.
With every prayer, a soft embrace,
We find our rest in boundless grace.

In valleys low, when fears consume,
A flicker shines, dispelling gloom.
In every trial, a lesson learned,
With every heart, a soul is turned.

Though eyes may fail to see the way,
A steadfast heart begins to sway.
Eternal truths like stars above,
Light our path with endless love.

So let us stand, though winds may howl,
For in the dark, we hear the soul.
Unseen waves of faith will guide,
In every heart, love will abide.

Dreams Forged in Silence

In quiet moments, dreams take flight,
In stillness, they embrace the night.
Whispers soft, where few may tread,
Hope blooms forth, where fears are shed.

Each fleeting thought, a seed of grace,
In solitude, we find our space.
The heart, a canvas, pure and wide,
Paints the visions deep inside.

With gentle hands, we sculpt our fate,
Crafting dreams, we elevate.
Each silent wish, a prayer in guise,
Forged in silence, they arise.

As dawn ignites the morning sky,
Fears dissolve, like clouds that fly.
With faith, we chase the bright-filled gleam,
For every soul deserves to dream.

So hold the silence, let it sing,
For in this hush, our spirits spring.
With every breath, let dreams enhance,
In quietude, we find our chance.

The Strength of Quiet Trust

In murmurs soft, a strength lies near,
In stillness true, we cast our fear.
Trust blooms quietly, like flowers born,
In fields of doubt, the heart's adorn.

Through trials faced and burdens shared,
In gentle whispers, we are bared.
With open hearts, we lean and bend,
Our quiet trust, a faithful friend.

Though noise may clash and tempests roar,
A steadfast spirit, we restore.
In moments rare, when silence speaks,
Strength rises up, the soul it seeks.

So take a breath, embrace the calm,
In hidden strength, we find the balm.
With quiet trust, we stand as one,
Together bound, till day is done.

In every heart, the light will shine,
With trust unwavering, faith divine.
Inside the stillness, power grows,
In quiet trust, our spirit flows.

A Prayer wrapped in Stillness

In gentle hush, a prayer unfolds,
Wrapped in silence, secrets hold.
Each earnest word, a sacred sigh,
Carried softly to the sky.

With every breath, we seek the grace,
In tranquil moments, we find our place.
Hands uplifted, hearts laid bare,
In stillness deep, we're held in care.

In shadows cast by days gone by,
A flicker bright, a whispered cry.
The soul speaks out, with love adorned,
Through silence, bonds of faith are formed.

So let us pause, and hear the call,
In every silence, we stand tall.
A prayer wrapped softly, pure and true,
Finds its way, to me and you.

With open hearts, we join the throng,
In stillness shared, we grow strong.
For in this space, divine will we trace,
A prayer of love, our souls embrace.

In Silence, a Shout

In the stillness of the night,
Whispers rise from hearts of light.
A prayer woven through the dark,
Echoes softly, leaves its mark.

Voices tremble, yet they soar,
Each word a plea, a spirit's roar.
In shadows deep, where fears reside,
Hope ignites, and faith won't hide.

With every breath, a promise made,
Through quiet moments, love displayed.
In silence, strength begins to grow,
A sacred power, pure as snow.

Lifted hands, though still they seem,
Create a symphony, a dream.
Every sigh, a seed that's sown,
In silence, we are not alone.

So let the whispers rise above,
Carried on waves of endless love.
In silent shouts, we find our way,
Guided by the light of day.

The Hidden Strength of a Prayer

In whispered thoughts, we find our might,
Entwined in grace, through day and night.
In humble hearts, a spirit stirs,
A hidden strength, like silent purrs.

Each word a stone against the tide,
With faith as anchor, we abide.
In fervent dreams, we softly kneel,
A force unknown, yet so revealed.

Through trials faced, we speak our hope,
In darkest hours, we learn to cope.
A sacred bond, unseen yet near,
The hidden strength of every prayer.

As dawn breaks bright, the shadows flee,
We stand in light, forever free.
Embraced by love, the spirit glows,
In each small prayer, true power flows.

So whisper softly, let love throng,
In every heart, we all belong.
With steadfast will, together we share,
The quiet strength found in a prayer.

Grace Under the Surface

Beneath the waves of life's fierce sea,
Lies grace as deep as love can be.
With every challenge, peace awaits,
A stillness found where fear abates.

In tempest storms, our souls may bend,
Yet through the trials, we transcend.
In every tear, a lesson clear,
Our spirits bloom, we persevere.

Through layers thick, our hearts will learn,
To shine with wisdom, fiercely burn.
In silence deep, each soul takes flight,
With grace beneath, we find the light.

Though shadows cross, and doubts may creep,
We stand with strength, our hearts will leap.
In humble trust, we rise anew,
With grace unbound, our joys accrue.

So let us draw from depths below,
The hidden grace that helps us grow.
With faith as anchor, pure and bright,
We dance above, a wondrous sight.

The Quietude that Protects

In tranquil moments, shadows blend,
A peaceful heart can surely mend.
With every breath, we guard the soul,
In quietude, we feel the whole.

Beneath the chaos of the day,
A shelter built where spirits sway.
In stillness found, the heart connects,
With greater truths that life reflects.

A soft embrace, a silent prayer,
In quietude, we find our care.
Where worldly noise begins to fade,
Our inner light will not be swayed.

Through gentle peace, we shield our way,
In every moment, let us stay.
Protected here, our spirits rise,
In quietude, we touch the skies.

The noise may tempt, but we are strong,
United in a sacred song.
With faith as guard, we gently tread,
In quietude, our souls are fed.

In the Quiet Embrace

In the stillness, hearts align,
Whispers of grace, a holy sign.
Through shadows cast by doubt and fear,
God's love surrounds, forever near.

With every breath, let spirits soar,
In silent prayer, we find the door.
A sacred bond, in peace we dwell,
In the quiet, all is well.

When storms arise, and tempests roar,
His gentle voice we can't ignore.
In trials faced, we hear Him call,
In the quiet, we stand tall.

With hearts attuned to heaven's song,
In unity, we remain strong.
In every moment, blessed and bright,
In the quiet, we find light.

So let us gather, hand in hand,
In this sacred, promised land.
Underneath His watchful eye,
In the quiet, we will fly.

Anchor of the Soul

In seas of doubt, when troubles rise,
You are the anchor, Lord, so wise.
Through waves of pain, through storms that shake,
Your love, our refuge, will not break.

With every trial, we stand as one,
In faith, our battles are well won.
A beacon shining through the night,
You guide our hearts, our souls take flight.

In moments bleak, when light feels lost,
You bear our burdens, no matter the cost.
Your whispers fall like gentle rain,
In Your embrace, we break the chain.

With joy we rise, with hope we stand,
In every prayer, we feel Your hand.
No fear remains when You are near,
Our anchor strong, our purpose clear.

So let us trust through thick and thin,
With You, dear Lord, our journey begins.
In every heartbeat, in every goal,
You are the anchor of the soul.

Beneath the Searing Sun

Beneath the sun, where shadows fade,
We seek Your comfort, unafraid.
In every challenge, in every trial,
Your grace empowers, makes us smile.

When burdens weigh like heavy stone,
In Your embrace, we are not alone.
You guide our steps with gentle hand,
Through desert paths, across the land.

In fields of gold, where hope is sown,
We find the joy that's purely grown.
With every whisper from above,
We're filled with strength and boundless love.

Though scorching days may test our might,
Your presence brings eternal light.
We walk with faith, through heat and rain,
In every moment, we'll sustain.

So let us lift our voices high,
In praise to You, O Lord on high.
In every heartbeat, in every run,
We find our peace beneath the sun.

The Veil of Tranquility

Behind the veil, where stillness lies,
We seek Your face, with longing eyes.
In gentle whispers, secrets told,
Within our hearts, Your love unfolds.

Through trials faced, through hearts that ache,
In Your sweet presence, fear will break.
A tranquil stream, a sacred space,
In every moment, feel Your grace.

Upon the mount, in quiet prayer,
We breathe in peace, let go of care.
Each prayer a thread, woven in trust,
In You we stand, in faith we must.

In shadows deep, Your light will shone,
Through darkened paths, we're never alone.
With hands uplifted, hearts relent,
In the veil of love, we're truly sent.

So let us gather, souls entwined,
In silence deep, Your peace we find.
Through every trial, through every plea,
In the veil of tranquility.

The Soft Roar of Enduring Love

In the whispers of dawn, love speaks clear,
Binding our souls with a thread so dear.
Through trials and storms, it shines bright,
A beacon of hope in the darkest night.

Hands held in prayer, hearts beat as one,
With every breath, a battle is won.
In laughter and tears, love's journey flows,
A river of grace, where compassion grows.

In the warmth of the sun, in the rain's gentle kiss,
We find in each moment, a glimpse of bliss.
Rooted in faith, we rise from despair,
For love's soft roar is always there.

In the echo of hearts, love's anthem sings,
With faith as our anchor, we spread our wings.
No distance too great, no darkness too deep,
In the arms of the Divine, our spirits leap.

Forever entwined, our paths align,
Each heartbeat a promise, eternally thine.
In love's sanctuary, we find our place,
United in purpose, enveloped in grace.

Surrendering to Sacred Silence

In the stillness of twilight, we pause to pray,
Releasing our burdens, letting them sway.
The world fades away in a sacred embrace,
We find in the silence, a holy space.

With each breath, we enter the deep,
Where whispers of wisdom begin to seep.
In the quietude, our spirits ignite,
Illuminated paths in the cloak of night.

We surrender our worries to the Divine,
In the arms of silence, our hearts align.
As the stars begin to twinkle and shine,
We lose ourselves in the sacred design.

With gentleness woven through every thought,
The echoes of love in the stillness caught.
In surrender, we trust the unseen flow,
Guided by light, as we let go.

Awake in the moment, enveloped in grace,
The beauty of silence, a soft, warm embrace.
We carry the peace beyond the day's end,
In the hymn of stillness, our hearts transcend.

The Sacred Breath of Inner Peace

Inhale the beauty, exhale the strife,
Each breath a blessing, a gift of life.
In the quiet of chaos, we find our ground,
The pulse of creation in stillness resounds.

With every heartbeat, harmony sings,
Awakening light in the simplest things.
In the depths of our souls, tranquility flows,
Where love is a river, and kindness grows.

Wrapped in the arms of the breath we take,
Unraveling burdens, the essence we make.
In the dance of existence, we learn to see,
The sacredness woven in you and in me.

Through the storms of the heart, the calm we find,
With courage and patience, our spirits aligned.
In the tapestry of life, peace is the thread,
Binding the living with all that is said.

With gratitude flowing, our hearts open wide,
In the sanctuary of breath, we reside.
Embracing the moment, we dwell in ease,
In the sacred rhythm of inner peace.

The Unfurling Wings of Faith

In the dawn of belief, we lift our gaze,
With hearts wide open, we sing our praise.
Each step we take, on the path so true,
Is a dance with the Divine, constantly new.

Like eagles soaring through skies of grace,
We embrace the journey, our sacred place.
With faith as our compass, we venture forth,
Exploring the depths of our spiritual worth.

In trials faced, we rise and stand tall,
Trusting the whispers that guide through it all.
The valleys of doubt, we navigate clear,
For faith is the anchor that draws us near.

With wings unfurled, we embrace the unknown,
In the arms of surrender, our spirits have grown.
Together, we journey through night into day,
With hope lighting paths where shadows may play.

In the chorus of life, our voices unite,
With fervor and passion, we shine our light.
The unfurling wings of faith take their flight,
As we journey together, hearts burning bright.

The Resilient Seed

In darkness deep, the seed is found,
A promise held beneath the ground.
With faith it breaks, the soil it seeks,
Emerging life, in whispered peaks.

The storm may rage, the winds may howl,
Yet still it stands, the roots do grow.
Through trials faced, it learns to bend,
In humble strength, it will ascend.

The sun, it shines on many days,
A guiding light through misty haze.
With patience soft, it reaches wide,
A testament of life inside.

From little things, great hopes arise,
The seedling stretches toward the skies.
In every heart, a dream is sown,
With love and grace, we are not alone.

So let us nurture what is small,
With gentle hands, we hearken the call.
For in each soul, a seed must grow,
To bring forth life, and love we show.

Finding Power in Stillness

Within the silence, peace does dwell,
A sacred space, where hearts compel.
In quiet breaths, we find our song,
A whispered truth, where we belong.

The world may spin in frantic pace,
Yet in stillness, we find grace.
Each moment still, a gift anew,
Revealing light that shines so true.

Beneath the rush, a deeper flow,
Our spirits rise, in tranquil glow.
In mindful breaths, the soul takes flight,
A dance of love in endless night.

To find the power, let go of fears,
Embrace the calm, release the tears.
For in this hush, we hear the call,
A silent strength that lifts us all.

So cherish moments, small and grand,
In stillness, let your spirit stand.
With each soft breath, the heart ignites,
In tranquil light, we seek new heights.

The Sacred Breath of Resolve

In every breath, a vow is made,
A sacred promise, never to fade.
With each inhale, we find our trust,
In exhale, strength from hope and dust.

The air we share, a gift divine,
With every heartbeat, grace entwined.
Resilience grows in trials faced,
In whispered prayers, our souls embraced.

Each moment lived, a chance to rise,
To lift the heart and clear the skies.
In sacred breath, we find our grace,
A holy light in time and space.

With every struggle, courage blooms,
As faith's sweet fragrance fills the rooms.
In sacred resolve, we walk the way,
With guiding light through night and day.

So breathe in deep, let worries cease,
In every moment, find your peace.
With sacred breath, our spirits soar,
In love united, forevermore.

The Fortress of the Spirit

Within our hearts, a fortress stands,
Built strong by love and sacred hands.
Through trials faced and storms we bear,
In unity, we find our care.

The walls are high, yet windows wide,
To let in light, and let love bide.
With faith as bricks, our hope shall rise,
A shelter safe beneath the skies.

Through every tear, the spirit grows,
In every joy, the love it knows.
A mighty shield against the night,
In harmony, we find our light.

Though winds may blow and shadows creep,
Our fortress stands, our faith runs deep.
In every heart, a guardian found,
With love's embrace, forever bound.

So let us gather, hand in hand,
Together strong, we make our stand.
In this great fortress, we shall thrive,
In love and hope, we stay alive.

The Still Light of Being

In the quiet dawn, a gentle glow,
Whispers of grace in the soft meadow.
Lifted in stillness, the spirit soars,
Bathed in the light that the heavens pour.

Each step we take on this sacred land,
Guided by faith, we know we stand.
Bound by the love in each tender beam,
Awakening hearts to the infinite dream.

In every shadow, a promise shines,
Illuminated pathways, divine designs.
With every breath, the soul ignites,
Embraced by the stillness of infinite lights.

Together we walk, hand in hand,
Drawn by the spark of a mighty plan.
United in purpose, our spirits blend,
In the still light of being, we transcend.

Embrace the journey, let it unfold,
Find wisdom and courage in tales untold.
For in the silence, the truth will sing,
Revealing the still light that existence brings.

Silent Echoes of Trust

In the heart's quiet, a promise lies,
Whispers of faith in the starlit skies.
With every heartbeat, we silently vow,
To rise above doubt, here and now.

Moments of stillness, where shadows fade,
Softly we listen as silence invades.
Trust in the journey, though paths may bend,
In the silent echoes, we find our mend.

With grace we walk through the muted night,
Holding the torch of a guiding light.
Each step, a testament to the love we've known,
In trusting the silence, we are never alone.

The whispers of ages embrace us tight,
In lessons of patience, our spirits ignite.
For in the stillness, we learn to be free,
In the silent echoes, we find our decree.

Let go of fear, and allow hope to rest,
In the quiet spaces, hearts are blessed.
For every heartbeat is a sign we've grown,
In the silent echoes, we're never on our own.

The Shield Crafted in Solitude

In solitude's arms, I find my peace,
A sanctuary built, where fears cease.
Each moment embraced, a sacred shield,
In stillness I gather the strength revealed.

The world may roar with tempestuous might,
But within, there blooms a calm, pure light.
Fortified spirits in moments alone,
Crafting my armor, where blessings are sown.

With every prayer, a layer is forged,
Buffeted storms, yet I'm never gorged.
In quiet reflection, the heart's resolve,
In solitude's haven, true selves evolve.

Hands raised in thanks for the solitude found,
In the quiet corners, my truths resound.
For in the making of my own inner space,
I wield the shield of divine grace.

Let the world turn, let the tempests rage,
In the solace of stillness, I turn the page.
With a heart now steadfast, and courage in sight,
In solitude's craft, I embrace the light.

The Integrity of the Heart

In the chambers of truth, the heart lays bare,
A canvas of conscience, woven with care.
Each beat a lesson, each sigh a prayer,
In the integrity of the heart, we share.

With kindness woven through every deed,
Compassion ignites in the silent need.
For hearts that unite in love's gentle art,
Become the beacon of the world's heart.

In the face of shadows, we hold our ground,
With integrity's voice, a melody found.
Each honest whisper, a guiding star,
Leading us onward, no matter how far.

With grace we tread on this sacred soil,
In the strength of our love, we endlessly toil.
For when we live true, and never depart,
We wrap the world in the integrity of the heart.

So rise, dear souls, let your spirits align,
In the warmth of your essence, let every light shine.
For in the dance of life, pure and smart,
We celebrate together the integrity of the heart.

Pillars of Hope in the Shadows

In the night where silence reigns,
The pillars rise, strong and true.
Whispers of faith, they sustain,
Guiding lost souls to renew.

Through valleys dark, where doubts reside,
Hope glimmers faint but ever bright.
With every step, the heart must bide,
In shadows, we find our light.

These steadfast arms, they hold the weight,
Embracing dreams that dare to breathe.
In the stillness, we wait,
For miracles hidden beneath.

A beacon shines through stormy weather,
Casting warmth on weary hearts.
In love's embrace, we are tethered,
Creating beauty in the parts.

So when the night begins to fall,
Remember, hope's not far away.
With every step, we heed the call,
Together we'll find the way.

The Gentle Surge of Introspective Light

In the stillness of the dawn,
A gentle light begins to rise.
Thoughts like rivers move along,
Reflecting truth in azure skies.

With every breath, the soul ignites,
Illuminated by love's grace.
Facing shadows, hearts unite,
Finding strength in each embrace.

The quiet urge, a faithful guide,
Leading us through paths unknown.
With every doubt, we cast aside,
In faith, our hearts are sown.

Embrace the journey, take the leap,
For in the depth, there lies the spark.
In moments cherished, softly weep,
For in the light, we find the dark.

So rise and let your spirit soar,
With introspection, seek and find.
In every heartbeat, seek for more,
A gentle surge that frees the mind.

Roots Deep in the Silent Soil

In hidden depths, where silence reigns,
The roots entwine beneath the ground.
In quiet strength, the heart maintains,
A bond unbroken, love unbound.

From shadows deep, the spirit grows,
Nourished by faith's gentle hand.
Through storms and trials, wisdom flows,
In unity, we firmly stand.

Branches stretch toward the heavens,
Reaching high, embracing light.
In every struggle, grace is given,
Transforming darkness into sight.

With each new season, life expands,
As hope renews the sacred soil.
Together weaving, hand in hands,
In harmony, we toil.

So let the roots hold fast and true,
In sacred ground, we find our way.
For every ending births anew,
In silent soil, we shall stay.

The Fortress Built on Faith

In the heart of every storm,
A fortress stands, resilient, bold.
Each brick laid down, a sacred form,
Constructed with a love untold.

Walls fortified by the trust we share,
In times of trial, they do not crack.
Through shadows thick, we show our care,
In faith's embrace, we find the track.

Together we weather every gale,
Holding on to promises made.
With courage, we shall prevail,
In every challenge, undismayed.

The gates are open, welcoming all,
With arms outstretched and eyes that see.
In unity, we rise and call,
Defenders of love's decree.

So let the storms rage high and fierce,
For inside, we stand, forever strong.
In every heart, faith's voice will pierce,
A fortress built where we belong.

The Unshaken Spirit's Prayer

O Lord, in trials I stand tall,
My spirit unshaken, I heed Your call.
Through shadows that creep and darkness near,
In faith, I rise, dispelling fear.

With each breath, I seek Thy grace,
In silent moments, I find my place.
A beacon of light, Your love anew,
In the depth of night, I trust in You.

When storms may rage and tempest roar,
I anchor my heart on the sacred shore.
For in the chaos, Your voice I hear,
Whispering peace, dispelling despair.

Grant me the strength to carry forth,
To spread Your love, my true life's worth.
In every challenge, in every trial,
I walk in faith, and I do not recoil.

O guide my spirit, let it be free,
In moments of doubt, remind me of Thee.
Together we rise, forever we sing,
In the arms of Heaven, my soul takes wing.

Beneath the Still Waters of Grace

In still waters, my soul finds rest,
Beneath waves of grace, I am truly blessed.
Your presence, Lord, a gentle stream,
In the quiet moments, I dwell and dream.

Ripples of love flow serene and wide,
Casting away all fear and pride.
In the depths of calm, Your whispers flow,
Nurturing faith, allowing it to grow.

The sun will rise, the dawn will break,
In Your embrace, no heart will ache.
For every tear, a promise made,
In every sorrow, Your light won't fade.

Brush away the doubts that bind,
In the stillness, a peace I find.
With every heartbeat, a prayer unfolds,
Trusting in grace, my spirit holds.

So let me float on waters wide,
Beneath Your wings, I shall abide.
In this sacred space, I am renewed,
Here in Your love, I am pursued.

Echoes of a Solitary Song

In solitude, I find my voice,
A melody sweet, in heart, rejoice.
With every note, a prayer I weave,
In echoes of love, I truly believe.

The wind carries whispers of hope,
In valleys deep, I learn to cope.
For each silence, a lesson learned,
In solitude's grace, my spirit yearned.

Mountains stand tall, shadows may loom,
Yet within my heart, there blooms a tune.
With every step, a sacred dance,
In the rhythm of faith, I seize my chance.

Though alone, I am never apart,
For in this journey, You hold my heart.
With each chord played, my spirit takes flight,
In echoes resounding, I find my light.

So let the solitary song resound,
Through valleys and hills, let love abound.
For in the silence, Your voice I hear,
Guiding my path, erasing fear.

The Unbroken Will of the Soul

Through trials fierce, my will runs strong,
In every struggle, I know I belong.
With steadfast heart, I journey forth,
In faith unshaken, I find my worth.

Each mountain climbed, each valley low,
In the depths of pain, I hear You flow.
A whisper of hope through darkness and strife,
Your love fuels my unbroken life.

With open arms, I face the storm,
For in Your presence, I am warm.
In shadows deep, Your light reveals,
A strength within, my soul it heals.

When doubts assail, I stand my ground,
In Your promises, my peace is found.
With every heartbeat, I rise anew,
For the will of my soul is rooted in You.

So guide my path, O Lord divine,
In every challenge, let Your glory shine.
For through it all, my spirit shall thrive,
With an unbroken will, I am alive.

Sacred Breath Amid the Noise

In the hush where whispers dwell,
I find the peace, a silent bell.
The world may roar, but here I stand,
In sacred breath, held by His hand.

Amid the chaos, hearts align,
In every pause, His love I find.
His gentle voice, a melody,
That soothes the soul and sets it free.

Cries of the world, I cast aside,
In faith I walk, my heart the guide.
With every breath, divinity,
Awakening my spirit's plea.

The sacred spark ignites the night,
Within the dark, He's the true light.
Though heavy clouds may block the sky,
In sacred breath, I learn to fly.

So breathe in deep, the holy air,
And let it weave away despair.
For in each breath, His love will grow,
A sacred bond that we both know.

The Power You Cannot Hear

In silence dwells a mighty force,
A whisper leads, it charts the course.
Though eyes may see, the heart must feel,
The power of love, the spirit's seal.

Within the stillness, voices rise,
Unseen, they leave the brightest prize.
A faith unmeasured, vast and true,
In every heartbeat, whispers new.

Though doubt may cloud the weary mind,
In trust we seek, and joy we find.
For in the dark, His presence glows,
A strength unseen, where spirit flows.

The thunder rolls, yet I remain,
In faith, I walk through doubt and pain.
For in the clash, my heart will soar,
On wings of hope, forevermore.

Listen deeply, for truth will sound,
Beyond the storm, love's pulse is found.
The power leads with gentle grace,
In silence, our souls embrace.

The Calm Within the Tempest

When waves crash hard upon the shore,
And thunder shakes, what goes before.
In chaos veiled, a peace is born,
A calm that fills my heart, reborn.

Though storms may rush and winds may wail,
I stand my ground, I will not fail.
For deep within, a whisper sings,
Of strength and hope, the peace it brings.

The tempest howls, yet in my chest,
There lies a sacred place of rest.
With every breath, the storm subsides,
In quiet trust, my faith abides.

Against the tide, my spirit swims,
In darkest night, His light still beams.
For storms may rage and skies may weep,
Yet in my heart, His promise keeps.

Be still, my soul, embrace the night,
For in the dark, there shines a light.
The tempest bows to quiet grace,
In every calm, I find His face.

Beneath the Tranquil Surface

Beneath the calm, a river flows,
Through shadows deep, where no one knows.
In stillness found, the spirit stirs,
And whispers hope, where silence purrs.

The outer world may seem to fade,
Yet in this space, His love is laid.
With every pulse, it speaks of grace,
Beneath the calm, I find my place.

The gentle waves, they kiss the shore,
As faith awakens, deepens more.
The stillness holds a sacred truth,
A promise bold, a fountain of youth.

So let the waters cleanse my soul,
In tides of love, I become whole.
For under waves, His peace abides,
In tranquil depths, the spirit glides.

I journey forth, with heart aflame,
In faith, I whisper, in His name.
Beneath the tranquil surface lies,
A world reborn, where beauty flies.

The Resolute Seed Beneath the Soil

In darkness deep, the seed does sleep,
With faith as roots, it holds the keep.
A gentle rain, a whispered prayer,
Awakens dreams from earth's own lair.

It burrows deep, through stone and clay,
In silence strong, it finds the way.
To pierce the shroud of earthly blight,
And greet the dawn with purest light.

Though trials come, and storms may rage,
The resolute seed will turn the page.
With heart so bold, it breaks the mold,
In every crack, its story told.

From humble earth, it climbs so high,
Reaching the bounds of vast, bright sky.
Each leaf unfurls, a testament,
To strength in faith, and love well-spent.

As petals bloom, behold the grace,
Of life's rebirth, in sacred space.
The seed once lost, now stands so tall,
Embracing truths that answer call.

The Whisper of Sacred Resilience

In quiet nights, a prayer descends,
A whisper soft, where silence bends.
Resilience grows where shadows loom,
Through aching hearts, it finds its room.

The soul's soft light, a lantern's glow,
Guides weary feet through pain and woe.
In every trial, a truth to glean,
A sacred strength in what has been.

With gentle hands, the Spirit weaves,
A tapestry of hope that cleaves.
Through wounds and scars, the heart expands,
Embracing love with open hands.

The beauty lies in struggles faced,
Each bruise and tear, a gift embraced.
In sacred whispers, trust shall grow,
With every breath, a seed to sow.

So rise, dear soul, in faith renew,
For whispers strong will carry you.
In harmony, we find our way,
Through night to dawn, to brightest day.

Triumphs on Worn Soles

With worn-out shoes, we pave the path,
Each step a dance, in grace we laugh.
Through trials faced and burdens borne,
The spirit's strength shall be reborn.

In dusty miles, our stories weave,
Of faith and hope that we believe.
Each crack beneath reflects the strife,
Yet blooms the beauty that is life.

As sacred journeys stretch the soul,
We find the light that makes us whole.
With every step, the heart does soar,
For in each trial, we learn once more.

The ground we tread, a hallowed place,
Where dreams take flight and trials race.
The joy of land, of sky, of sea,
In worn-out shoes, the heart is free.

So march on forth, through dusk and dawn,
For triumph lives where love is drawn.
With every sole that kisses earth,
Awake the magic of rebirth.

The Unvoiced Fight for the Divine

In silent battles, hearts collide,
Where faith and doubt in shadows hide.
The unvoiced fight, a sacred quest,
In deepest calm, we seek our rest.

Each breath a prayer, a gentle plea,
For strength to rise, to simply be.
As whispers sing from deep within,
We dare to face the noise of sin.

Though storms may rage, and tempests cry,
The spirit stirs, we reach for sky.
In quiet corners, truths ignite,
And in the dark, we find the light.

With every heartbeat, courage grows,
A flame that burns, a love that glows.
In battles lost, and victories won,
The path will shine, our souls as one.

So take your stand, in faith abide,
For in the depths, our hearts confide.
The unvoiced fight for the Divine,
Awakens love in every line.

Uncharted Paths of Stealthy Grace

In shadows deep, the spirit walks,
Guided by whispers, where silence talks.
Each step a prayer, a heart's embrace,
On uncharted paths of stealthy grace.

The stars alight with a sacred glow,
Revealing truths that we may not know.
In hidden realms, the faithful find,
A journey woven by the Divine mind.

With every challenge, faith ignites,
In moments of doubt, grace reunites.
Through valleys low, to mountains high,
The spirit soars, unafraid to fly.

In the unseen, a light will shine,
For every heart that seeks to align.
In quiet trust, the soul will trace,
The uncharted paths of stealthy grace.

In the Stillness, Hope Awakens

In the stillness, where voices fade,
Hope awakens, unafraid.
In gentle whispers of the night,
Faith blooms softly, pure and bright.

As dawn breaks forth, a new refrain,
The sun's embrace, a balm for pain.
With every heartbeat, love takes flight,
In the stillness, grace ignites.

When burdens weigh like heavy chains,
In silence, peace remains.
Each tear that falls, a seed of trust,
In the stillness, hope is a must.

From silent depths, the spirit sings,
Of sacred truths that freedom brings.
As shadows flee and joy awakes,
In the stillness, hope remakes.

The Strength of the Unseen Path

Through trials faced, the spirit grows,
In whispered winds, the courage flows.
The strength of the unseen path,
Leads us through both wrath and wrath.

Beneath the storm, a heart holds fast,
The shadows fall, but faith will last.
With every step, we forge our way,
The unseen guides, come what may.

In unity, our voices rise,
Together bound, we reach the skies.
With love as our unfailing guide,
The strength of faith will turn the tide.

In moments dark, a spark will flare,
A light that shines when none will care.
For in the depths, our souls will laugh,
The strength of the unseen path.

Resplendent Quietude

In resplendent quietude, hearts align,
Where the sacred whispers intertwine.
Each breath a prayer, a soul's delight,
In the still of night, we find our light.

With every heartbeat, peace unfolds,
A tapestry of grace, in colors bold.
In solitude, our spirits dance,
In resplendent quietude, a second chance.

As nature's song plays soft and low,
In tranquil moments, love will grow.
With open hearts, we learn to see,
The beauty wrapped in humility.

The world may rush with frantic pace,
Yet here we find our sacred space.
In peace we dwell, embraced by fate,
In resplendent quietude, we celebrate.

Milton Keynes UK
Ingram Content Group UK Ltd.
UKHW020043271124
451585UK00012B/1027

9 789916 899311